TRIP & TOWN

ENJOY THE ATL
IN 2019!

Chris Harben

Atlanta

GEORGIA

A PHOTOGRAPHIC PORTRAIT

Photography by Chris Hamilton

Narrative by Sara Day

TWIN LIGHTS PUBLISHERS | ROCKPORT, MASSACHUSETTS

First published in the
United States of America by:

Twin Lights Publishers, Inc.
Rockport, Massachusetts 01966
Telephone: (978) 546-7398
www.twinlightspub.com

ISBN: 978-1-934907-58-0

10 9 8 7 6 5 4 3 2 1

(opposite)
Waterwall, Woodruff Park

(frontispiece)
Atlanta Skyline

(jacket front)
Modern Peach in the plaza of the
Georgia World Congress Center

(jacket back)
Centennial Olympic Park and
One Woman Rising in Freedom Park

Book design by:
SYP Design & Production, Inc.
www.sypdesign.com

Printed in China

With its unique blend of Southern charm and urban sophistication, the city of Atlanta has an indescribable electricity you can almost feel. From the affluent Buckhead neighborhood, to the glistening skyscrapers in Midtown, the distinct spark of this vibrant city is apparent through its art, culture, music, architecture, cuisine, and so much more. Nestled within a deep green forest, this is a world-class city unlike any other.

Atlanta was originally called Terminus for the southern terminus of a railroad that was built in 1837 at what is now Five Points. The name then changed to Marthasville and renamed Atlanta in 1845 for the Western Atlantic Railroad. Atlanta's development into a great metropolis was due primarily to the success of the railway industry. Nicknamed "The Gate City," Atlanta was established as a major thoroughfare from the East coast to the West once the railroads were completed in the mid-1800s. Today, it remains a major transportation hub, being home to Hartsfield-Jackson International Airport—the busiest airport in the world.

Railways were also an important part of the American Civil War and Atlanta, a major supply depot for the Confederacy. Its military significance made it a prime target and, in 1864, it was overcome by Union troops and burned to the ground. However, as its symbol of the mythological Phoenix rising from the ashes suggests, this battered city would persevere. Today, towering high rises, world-class museums, renowned education and research institutions, state-of-the-art convention centers, and professional sports venues are a testament to Atlanta's grit and steadfastness. A true urban success story, Atlanta would grow to become the capital of the new south—a premier city with boundless possibilities and capabilities favorable enough for it to host the Centennial Summer Olympic Games in 1996. Atlanta's ability to not only survive, but to thrive, is an irreproachable trait that is embedded deep within the spirit of those fortunate enough to call this place home.

A long line of Atlantans would continue to shape an entire country, from the courageous efforts of native Atlantan Dr. Martin Luther King, Jr., whose peaceful fight for civil rights would touch the lives of generations to come, to the literary genius of Margaret Mitchell, author of the epic tale, *Gone with the Wind*, and innovators like Coca-cola founder Asa Griggs Candler.

And notwithstanding a robust economical industry that has attracted several Fortune 1000 and Fortune 500 companies, Atlanta is also a place where residents and visitors alike can become one with nature. Its unique geographical location at the foothills of the Appalachian Mountains afford endless opportunities for outdoor activities. And its plentiful parks and green spaces throughout the city provide a peaceful respite from busy city life.

From its rich history, to its modern marvels, photographer Chris Hamilton has captured the very soul of Atlanta in this unparalleled collection of exquisite imagery.

Westin Peachtree Plaza (opposite)

Designed by John Portman, this massive, cylindrical hotel measures 188 feet in diameter and towers 73 stories above the streets of Atlanta. Opened in 1976, the iconic skyscraper features over 5,000 windows, glass elevators, and panoramic views from the Sun Dial Restaurant on the top floor.

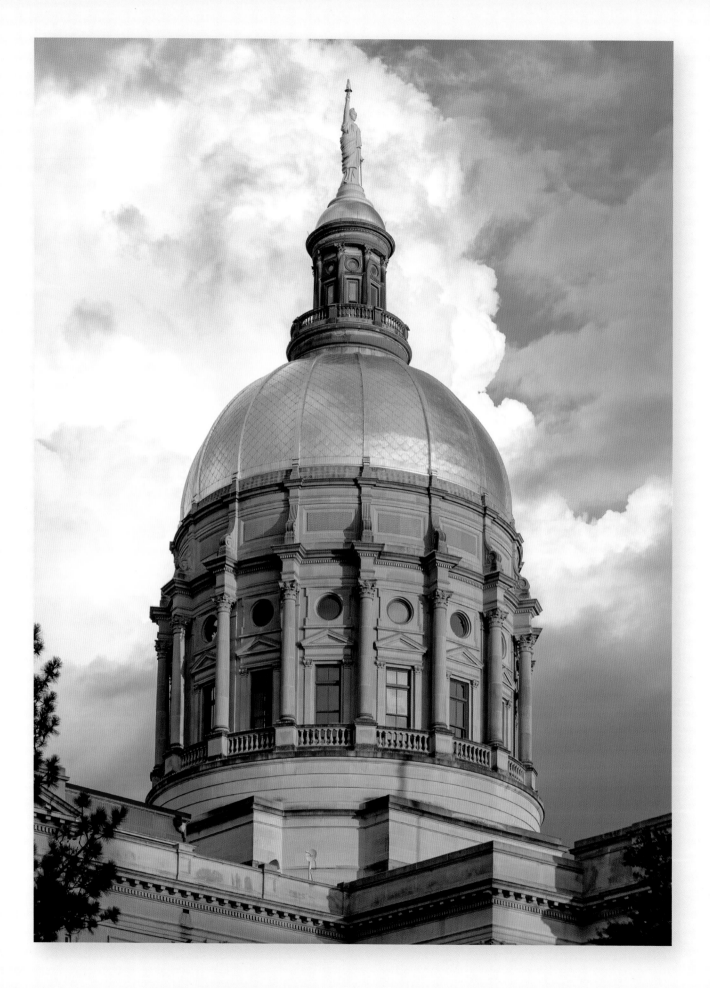

Georgia State Capitol

(above and opposite)

The gilded dome of the Georgia State Capitol is a striking landmark in the city's business district. The capital was moved to Atlanta in 1868 and the Neo-classical Renaissance Revival building has been the seat of state government since it was completed in 1889.

Atlanta Skyline *(top and bottom)*

Atlanta's skyline is distinctly different from its varied points of view. From the first high-rises of Colony Square in 1972, the skyline has sprouted into three major districts—Downtown, Midtown, and Buckhead. Atlanta is home to roughly 5.8 million people and several Fortune 500 and 1000 companies.

Carnegie Education Pavilion *(opposite)*

Located in Hardy Ivy Park, the Carnegie Education Pavilion was built from the marble façade of the former Carnegie Central Library, which was demolished in 1977. Designed by Henri Jova, the Beaux-Arts monument to education features the names of three poets, Aesop, Dante, Milton, and contributor, Carnegie.

SunTrust Plaza *(above and left)*

Originally named One Peachtree Center, this 60-story, postmodern high-rise was designed by John Portman and completed in 1992. Its unique design allows up to 36 corner offices per floor. One of several professional buildings that comprise the sprawling Peachtree Center Complex, it is the second tallest building in Atlanta.

Ballet Olympia *(opposite)*

A pair of 15-foot-tall, bronze dancers are entwined in a graceful flow of ribbons as they appear to prance along Peachtree Street in SunTrust Plaza. *Ballet Olympia* is an adaptation of the original sculpture, *Maenad*, by artist Paul Manship. Mythological "maenads" were inspired to dance passionately in a show of devotion to the Greek god Dionysus.

Millennium Gate Museum (above)

Located on a placid lake at Atlantic Station, the design and surrounds of the Millennium Gate Museum provide a peaceful respite among a bustling city. The arch features a Latin inscription that translates, *"This American monument is dedicated to all peaceful accomplishment, Anno Domini 2000."*

The Gate (opposite top)

Atlanta was dubbed "The Gate City" of the south when it became a major thoroughfare from the East coast to the West upon completion of the railroads in the mid-1800s. This magnificent, 100-foot-tall arch is a tribute to the peaceful contributions of innovators and pioneers of Georgia and beyond.

Preserving Georgia's History
(opposite bottom)

Completed in 2008, the 12,000-square-foot Millennium Gate Museum preserves Georgia's historic, cultural, and architectural accomplishments. Seven levels contain an extensive collection of art, artifacts, and exhibits throughout multiple galleries.

Atlantic Station *(above)*

Once the site of the Atlantic Steel Mill, this 138-acre site in Midtown has developed into a thriving, mixed-use environment. Residents and visitors can shop, dine, work, and play in this pedestrian-friendly destination. Established in 2005, it continues to grow and change with the needs of the community.

Bank of America Plaza *(left and opposite)*

Atlanta's tallest high-rise at 1,023 feet, (also tallest in the Southeastern United States), offers 1.3 million square feet of office space. Designed by Kevin Roche John Dinkeloo & Associates in 1992, the 55-story, steel and granite tower features a stunning, steel-framed pyramid that is topped with a 90-foot-tall, gold-leaf spire. The building is LEED Silver Certified for sustainability.

The Georgian Terrace *(above)*

The historic Georgian Terrace in Midtown opened in 1911 and is the official hotel of the Fox Theatre. Designed in the Beaux-Arts style by William Lee Stoddart, it is rich in architectural detail and has been visited by dignitaries such as F. Scott Fitzgerald, President Calvin Coolidge, and Walt Disney.

Atlanta from the Ashes *(right)*

Known as *The Phoenix*, a mythological bird that was consumed by fire and rose from the ashes, this 18-foot-tall, bronze monument stands as a tribute to a city that overcame the devastation of the Civil War to become a world-class metropolis. Located in Woodruff Park, the statue was dedicated in 1969.

Hurt Building *(opposite)*

Evoking historic southern charm, the triangular Hurt Building first opened in 1926. One of the city's first skyscrapers, its interior has undergone extensive renovation and, today, boasts many modern amenities, while its exterior retains its original design. It is listed on the National Register of Historic Places.

Piedmont Park

The skyline's reflection melds its early evening colors in the waters of Lake Clara Meer in Piedmont Park. The park consists of 180 acres of open space, including trails, playgrounds, ball fields, and tennis courts. Centrally located, the park hosts an array of summer festivals as well as the popular Green Market.

Metro Atlanta *(above and left)*

Mirrored surfaces with crisp edges reflect the distinct economic vibe of Atlanta's modern architectural landscape. Home to several Fortune 500/1000 companies, the city is well known for its opportunistic business environment. A leader in innovation, it has been voted number one for business by corporate peers.

SkyView Atlanta *(opposite)*

Taking in the sights from one of SkyView's 42 gondolas is a uniquely exhilarating experience. From historic neighborhoods to glistening skyscrapers and tree-canopied green spaces, this 20-story Ferris wheel, located in Centennial Park, provides breathtaking panoramas of downtown Atlanta.

Peachtree Street Bridge

Graceful, 30-foot-tall arches that span 240 feet, loop over pedestrian walkways on either side of the Peachtree Street Bridge. Part of a $6M beautification project, the bridge features 6-foot-tall letters which, when illuminated, become a stunning evening spectacle viewed from I-85 running beneath it.

Peachtree Center

An icon in downtown Atlanta, Peachtree Center is comprised of 6 high-rises connected by a series of skywalks that provide over 2 million square feet of office space, as well as three hotels, 50 restaurants, and a variety of shops.

Centennial Olympic Park

More than 20 years ago, a dismal
stretch of property was transformed
into a magnificent, 21-acre greenspace
that would serve as the main gathering
place for the 1996 Centennial Olympic
Games. Operated by the Georgia World
Congress Center Authority, today, it
serves as the public's urban oasis.

Fountain of Rings *(above and right)*

One of the most sophisticated fountains in the world, this refreshing landmark is the focal point of Centennial Olympic Park. Comprised of five interconnecting rings of the Olympic logo, it features a music show that plays four times a day with 251 synchronized jets spraying water up to 30 feet high.

Evening in Atlanta *(top)*

The illuminated SkyView Ferris wheel slowly revolves in Centennial Olympic Park. High above the city, spectators, comfortably contained within climate-controlled gondolas, take in fabulous sights, including the glowing pyramid atop the Bank of America building as it pierces the evening sky.

Olympic Cauldron Tower *(bottom)*

Perched atop a 132-foot-tall lookout tower, this 21-foot-tall cauldron is a tribute to the 1996 Centennial Olympic Games. In one of the events' most memorable moments, heavyweight champion boxer Muhammad Ali lit the flame, officially opening the games in which 197 countries would compete.

City in a Forest

Evening lights in Centennial Olympic Park paint a tranquil reflecting pool and surrounding trees with luminous color. Often referred to as the "city in a forest," Atlanta boasts the densest tree canopy of all major cities in the United States, with trees covering more than 30 percent of the city's 133-square-mile area.

The Atlanta Nine *(above and left)*

More than 20 years ago, a group of nine Atlanta business leaders embraced the concept of hosting the Olympic Games in their city and worked diligently to make that dream a reality. This monument in Centennial Olympic Park is a tribute to their spirited efforts that would reshape the city for decades to come.

William Porter "Billy" Payne *(opposite)*

With a firm grasp on an Olympic torch, this life-sized, bronze statue of William Porter "Billy" Payne, created by sculptor Shinzo Nobuhito Matoba, is located in Centennial Olympic Park. Payne, along with Andrew Young, was a visionary who brought the 1996 Olympic Games to Atlanta in 1996, catapulting the city into world-class status.

Flair Across America

Sculpted by artist Richard MacDonald and dedicated in 1996, *Flair Across America* is a tribute to the triumph of the human spirit. This 22-foot-tall, bronze statue journeyed across the U.S., visiting several cities before arriving at its final location at the Georgia World Congress Center.

Baron Pierre de Coubertin Statue

French scholar and historian Baron Pierre de Coubertin was responsible for reviving the Olympic Games in 1896. Created by American sculptor Raymond Kaskey, this monument, located in Centennial Olympic Park, is dedicated to his ambitious vision of the new Olympic Games we enjoy today.

Quilt of Origins *(above and left)*

Three runners, creatively embedded in a bronze arch, each represent the first Olympic Games in Olympia, Greece, in 776 BC; the Modern Games in Athens, Greece, in 1896, and the Centennial Games, in Atlanta, in 1996. Weighing more than eight tons, the arch, located in Centennial Olympic Park, is a tribute to the Games' Hellenic origin.

Paralympic Legacy *(opposite)*

Two weeks after the 1996 Centennial Olympic Games, 3,259 athletes from 104 countries participated in the Paralympic Games and set 269 world records here in Atlanta. Located in Centennial Olympic Park, the monument features four granite columns on which the names of the athletes are inscribed.

Modern Peach *(above)*

A gleaming, stainless-steel peach stands 27 feet tall in the plaza of the Georgia World Congress Center. Weighing five tons, the massive *Modern Peach*, by sculptor Gregory Johnson, celebrates the 50th season of college football's Peach Bowl and has become a popular photo-op backdrop as well.

Atlanta BeltLine Art *(left)*

Created by Atlanta artist and architect, Tim Frank, a granite seat surrounded by vertical columns provides an interesting resting spot for walkers, runners, and cyclists along Eastside Trail. Mimicking tall Georgia pine trees, the piece provides cool shade in summer and warmth from solar heat in winter.

World Athletes Monument *(opposite)*

Five stalwart figures, representing the five participating continents, uphold a bronze globe atop the 55-foot-tall, limestone World Athletes Monument in Midtown. Also known as Prince of Wales's Monument, it was gifted to the city in 1996 by Prince Charles, and stands as a tribute to international athletic competition.

Hartsfield-Jackson International Airport *(top and bottom)*

With over 100 million passengers per year traveling to more than 150 domestic and 75 international destinations, Hartsfield-Jackson is the busiest airport in the world. Built on the former Atlanta Speedway racetrack, today, it is a symbol of the city's economic prowess.

View from the Top *(opposite)*

Beyond the high-rises to tree-covered landscape and distant hills, Atlanta's metropolitan area spans more than 6,000 miles. Home to roughly 463,878 people within the city proper, and roughly 5.8 million in the metropolitan area, Georgia's capital continues to thrive.

Atlanta Streets (top)

Onlookers are riveted to a rollerblader as he seems to defy gravity during this challenging endeavor along Marietta Street. The Fairlie-Poplar District is a hip, revitalized neighborhood that is popular with students from Georgia State University, whose campus is located within the area.

Fairlie-Poplar District (bottom)

The Farlie-Poplar District was known as the "fireproof business district" after the Civil War when its buildings were reconstructed using stone, brick, and iron. Today, it's a trendy neighborhood with an energetic vibe. Galleries, theatres, restaurants, street art, and nightlife add to the draw.

Flatiron Building (opposite)

Built in 1897, this iconic, 11-story-tall office building was originally called the English-American Building. Now referred to as FlatIron City, renovations awarded it 2017 Project of the Year by the Urban Land Institute of Atlanta. The triangular, Neoclassic landmark is on the National Register of Historic Places.

Ponce City Market

Situated on 16 acres, this massive 2,100,000-square-foot behemoth was once home to Sears, Roebuck & Company. The historic building is the city's largest revitalization project which now includes residences, office space, shops, a gourmet food hall, and a rooftop amusement park.

Ponce City Market *(top and bottom)*

Located on Ponce de Leon Avenue, Ponce City Market officially opened in 2014. An ambitious transformation changed the historic Sears, Roebuck & Company building to a popular city destination, with shops, restaurants, farmers market, and exciting events throughout the year.

Cabbagetown (opposite)

Once an old textile mill settlement during the late 1800s, this artsy, East Atlanta neighborhood features colorful cottages, street art, and eateries with great Southern cuisine. The area's name origin differs, from early produce peddlers' ware, to a train derailment that covered the area with cabbages.

Little Five Points (top and bottom)

Tattoo parlors, vintage clothing shops, indie book stores, and hip ethnic eateries are all part of what makes this vibrant and eclectic neighborhood so alluring. Located in central downtown Atlanta, "L5P," with its offbeat, Bohemian flair, is likened to San Francisco's Haight-Ashbury neighborhood.

Old Fourth Ward *(top and bottom)*

Street artists leave a colorful mark in Atlanta's Old Fourth Ward neighborhood. This historic area is the birthplace of Dr. Martin Luther King, Jr. and home to Ebenezer Baptist Church and the Sweet Auburn District. It has fast become one of the city's happening hot spots for dining and nightlife.

Expressions *(top and bottom)*

Evidence of Atlanta's passion for public street art can be seen throughout its neighborhoods. Talented muralists convey ideas in an array of color and styles—telling stories of culture and history that paint a vibrant picture of Atlanta today and inspire the promise of a multicolored tomorrow.

Living Walls *(top and bottom)*

Bare city walls become the creative canvases of artists from all over the world who take part in the urban art conference, Living Walls. Here, Australian artist Fintan Magee, known for his environmentally and socially themed murals, adorns two walls with his signature levitating figures.

Atlanta Murals *(top and bottom)*

From the dynamic depiction of Dr. Martin Luther King, Jr. by Atlanta artist Fabian Williams to the blossoming garden by Detroit artist Louise Jones (Ouizi) that spurs new life to a building along the Beltline, Atlanta has been ranked one of America's best cities for street art by the *HuffPost*.

Center for Civil and Human Rights

Established in 2007 and opened to the public in 2014, the 42,000-square-foot Center for Civil and Human Rights is dedicated to the history and progression of human rights around the world. Located on Ivan Allen Jr. Boulevard, the center joins American civil rights movements with those worldwide.

Powerful Displays (top and bottom)

Exhibits at the Center for Civil and Human Rights are powerful tools that educate, empower, and enlighten. From the legacy of civil rights leader Dr. Martin Luther King, Jr. to ruthless world dictators, visitors gain understanding through stories of historic struggles that are told in bold detail.

Lessons from the Past *(top and bottom)*

Thoughtful exhibits at the Center for Civil and Human Rights display Atlanta's role in the American civil rights movement that transformed the nation and directed its future. Volatile social and political climates would take gradual and often painful paths to facilitate positive change.

Passage *(opposite)*

Inspirational quotes by Nelson Mandela and Margaret Mead are etched upon the glass walls of this 32-foot-tall monument outside the Center for Civil and Human Rights. Designed by Larry Kirkland, visitors can stroll beneath *Passage* and read these moving sentiments through cascading waters.

CNN Center *(above and left)*

Broadcasting world events from cutting-edge studios, Cable News Network (CNN) is headquartered in Atlanta. Guided tours provide a peek at the inner workings of a major network. The center also houses the Omni Hotel and the largest freestanding escalator in the world, at eight stories high and 196 feet long.

Georgia International Convention Center

Located at Gateway Center and directly connected to the airport via the ATL SkyTrain, the 400,000-square-foot GICC is the second largest convention center in the state. Atlanta's newest convention center, it features 3 hotels and a 40,000-square-foot ballroom.

Fox Theatre *(top)*

Fox Theatre opened in 1929 on Christmas Day when it presented Walt Disney's first cartoon, *Steamboat Willie*. Today, the venue hosts major Broadway shows and top entertainers. The 4,665-seat theatre includes "Mighty Moe," a 3,622-pipe Möller organ—the world's largest Möller theatre organ.

Fox Marquee Club *(bottom)*

Steeped in ornate Arabian ambiance, the 10,000-square-foot Fox Marquee Club adds a level of luxurious exclusivity to an evening at the theatre. Members enjoy upscale cuisine, signature Marquee cocktails, and access to rooftop terraces before, during, and after the show.

Fox Origins *(opposite)*

The historic Fox Theatre was originally intended to be a Shriners Temple. However, financial strain forced a handover to developer William Fox, who would transform it into an extravagant movie palace. With over 150 performances a year, it is one of the city's premiere entertainment venues.

Cobb Energy Performing Arts Centre
(above and opposite)

Opened in 2007, this premier performance venue features a 2,750-seat theatre and 10,000-square-foot ballroom. Home to the Atlanta Opera and the Atlanta Ballet, the building's 65-foot-tall glass wall and sweeping curve add drama to its sleek, modern design.

The Varsity *(right)*

From locals to dignitaries, The Varsity has been serving great food since 1928. Waiters greet with, "What'll ya have?!" and use lingo like *Bag of Rags* (chips) and *Walk a Dog* (hot dog to go). The Atlanta icon, famous for chili cheese dogs and orange drinks, is the largest drive-in restaurant in the world.

World of Coca-Cola *(top)*

From its original location in downtown, to the current Pemberton Place location, this popular attraction has welcomed over 24 million guests. It fills a 92,000-square-foot building with cola history, including interactive exhibits, theatre, the famous Coca-Cola polar bear, a working bottling line, and more.

Five Points *(bottom)*

A 48-foot-tall Coca-Cola sign glows atop the historic Olympic Building, lighting up the city's hub, better known as Five Points. Marietta Street, Edgewood Avenue, Decatur Street and two stretches of Peachtree Street converge at the city center, convenient to parks, offices, and public transportation.

Peachtree Street *(above)*

Margaret Mitchell penned *Gone with the Wind* and Coca-Cola was invented and first sold here at Atlanta's most prestigious address. Peachtree Street, the location of many historic and architecturally significant buildings, is also a predominate parade path and a stretch of the world's largest 10k running event, the AJC Peachtree Road Race.

Georgia-Pacific Building *(right)*

The natural hue of the buildings' pink granite façade intensifies in the light of the golden hour. Georgia-Pacific is headquartered in this 52-story tower that was built in 1982. Designed by architectural firm Skidmore, Owings & Merrill, its unique, stair-step shape is highlighted in the play of light and shadow.

Dazzling Display *(above)*

The city of Atlanta celebrates the nations' birthday with star-spangled events throughout the metropolitan area. Parades, barbecues, and concerts at Centennial Olympic Park, featuring Grammy-award-winning artists, culminate in a spectacular fireworks display—the largest in the Southeastern United States.

191 Peachtree Tower *(left)*

This 50-story-tall, postmodern office tower was once Atlanta's premier business address. The twin-tower design of granite and glass is topped with two recognizable crown structures—beautiful arches and domes that are illuminated at night. 191 Peachtree Tower is the fourth tallest high-rise in the city.

1180 Peachtree (above and right)

With gracefully tapered sides, clad in gleaming reflective glass, 1180 Peachtree is an award-winning sky-scraper in both design and sustainabil-ity. Located in Midtown, the 41-story tower was designed by architects Pickard-Chilton and is a stunning specimen along the skyline.

Peachtree Road Race *(above and left)*

The Atlanta Journal-Constitution (AJC) Peachtree Road Race is a popular Fourth of July event that draws approximately 60,000 participants, making it the world's largest 10k race. Organized by the Atlanta Track Club, the race is routed from Buckhead, through Midtown, and finishes at Piedmont Park.

Peachtree Road Race
Push-Assist Division

Wheelchair athletes team up with experienced long-distance runners in this highly competitive division of the Peachtree Road Race. These dynamic duos are sponsored by the Shepherd Center, the Atlanta Track Club, and partner with the Kyle Pease Foundation.

Decatur *(above and left)*

Between the city of Atlanta and historic Stone Mountain is the small college town of Decatur. Established in 1823 at the intersection of two Indian paths, Decatur is a chic destination known for its pedestrian-friendly, tree-lined streets and its locally owned shops, galleries, and restaurants.

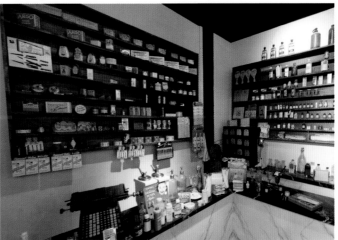

APEX Museum *(top and bottom)*

Founded in 1978, the African-American Panoramic Experience (APEX) explores the span of history from ancient Africa to present-day America. Located in Sweet Auburn, significant contributions are conveyed through exhibits and artifacts that delve into the history and culture of African Americans.

Prehistoric Marvels *(above)*

The world's largest dinosaurs lurk in the Great Hall of the Fernbank Museum of Natural History. The *Giants of the Mesozoic* exhibit features a massive 123-foot-long prehistoric Argentinosaurus being accosted by a 47-foot-long, razor-toothed Giganotosaurus, one of the largest carnivorous dinosaurs on earth.

Fernbank Museum of Natural History *(left)*

Opened in 1992, this esteemed natural history museum includes interactive permanent and special exhibits, films, outdoor exploration via WildWoods and Fernbank Forest trails, and more. Adults gather at Fernbank After Dark to enjoy live music, cocktails, and movies in the new Giant Screen Theater.

Michael C. Carlos Museum
(above and right)

Ancient treasures from Greece, Rome, Egypt, Asia, Africa, and the Americas draw thousands of history enthusiasts to Emory University's Michael C. Carlos Museum annually. Founded in 1919, this internationally acclaimed museum also features a teaching lab, educational programs, lectures, and workshops.

Preserving Ancient Egypt

The permanent collection of the
Michael C. Carlos Museum includes
extensive artifacts from Emory profes-
sor William A. Shelton's Egyptian excur-
sion in 1920. Since then, the collection
has expanded to include artifacts from
the 21st Dynasty (ca. 1070–946 BC) to
the Roman Period (ca. 31 BC–395 AD).

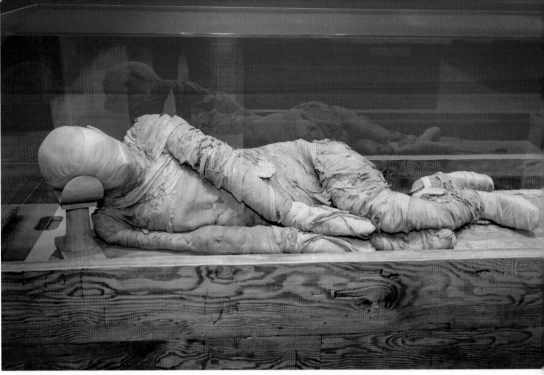

Early Mummification *(top)*

Dating back to 2305-2152 BC, a mummy, wrapped in frayed layers of linen at the Michael C. Carlos Museum, seems to be napping comfortably on its side. Bodies of Egyptians were preserved in sleeping positions until after the Old Kingdom (6th Dynasty) period, when they were buried lying flat.

A Collection to Behold *(bottom)*

Illustrated "coffin boards" were secondary lids that covered the well-preserved mummies lying beneath them. These ancient relics are ornately decorated with winged goddesses, epithets, and symbols of protection that were believed to guard the soul during its journey into the afterlife.

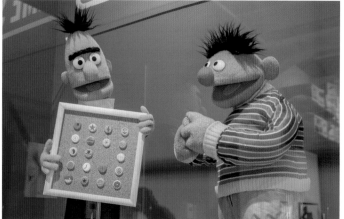

Center for Puppetry Arts

The award-winning Center for Puppetry Arts, located on the site of the former Spring Street Elementary School, was founded in 1978. Since its ribbon cutting by famed puppeteer Jim Henson, the center's delightful exhibits, events, and workshops have highlighted the history of puppetry from cultures around the world.

Children's Museum of Atlanta

With fun, interactive exhibits and educational programs, The Children's Museum of Atlanta is a place where kids can discover, learn, and imagine. Opened to the public in 2003, it also features *Museum-on-the-Go*, bringing art, science, culture, technology, and more into participating classrooms.

LEGOLAND® Discovery Center

Pirate Adventure Island is one of several attractions at LEGOLAND® Discovery Center. The Kingdom Quest laser ride, 4D cinema, workshops, and activities make for a day of creative fun for kids of all ages. A Discovery Center app helps to plan a visit, participate in a Scavenger Hunt, or check upcoming events.

MINILAND®

The streets of Atlanta come to life at LEGOLAND® Discovery Center's *MINI-LAND*® exhibit. This fascinating display features the city's most recognizable skyscrapers and landmarks, working cars and trains, and more—all created in minute detail using over 1.5 million colorful LEGO® bricks.

Georgia Aquarium

The ship-like façade of the Georgia Aquarium invites visitors to explore a captivating undersea world. With more than 10 million gallons of water housing over 100,000 animals, it's one of the world's largest aquariums. It was gifted to the city by Bernie Marcus, co-founder of The Home Depot.

Ocean Voyager *(top and bottom)*

Whale sharks, manta rays, goliath grouper, and thousands of other animals are observed through the enormous acrylic windows of Georgia Aquarium's Ocean Voyager exhibit—one of the largest aquatic exhibits in the world. The aquarium is renowned for its dedication to animals both here and in the wild.

The Art of Sound (above)

Sonic Playground at the High Museum of Art invites visitors to experience the art of sound with this interactive sculpture by renowned Japanese artist, Yuri Suzuki. Installed on Sifly Piazza in 2018 as part of the Piazza Activation Initiative that brings art to the outdoors, the colorful flower and bell shapes produce sounds in playful variations.

High Museum of Art (left)

Auguste Rodin's ca. 1880 sculpture, *The Shade*, contrasts the museum's bright white exterior. Growing extensively since its founding in 1905, the High Museum of Art has a permanent collection of over 15,000 works including American, European, African American, modern art, and photography.

Woodruff Arts Center

Comprised of the Alliance Theatre, Atlantic Symphony Orchestra, and the High Museum of Art, the Woodruff Arts Center encompasses an area of over 900,000 square feet. An Atlanta staple for half a century, it is also the largest arts education facility in the state, with over 200,000 students.

Museum of Contemporary Art
(top and bottom)

Contemporary artists from Georgia and around the world are showcased in exhibits throughout the year at MOCA. Founded in 2000, the museum is renowned for keeping in touch with the community through engaging artist talks and public programs.

Museum of Design *(top and bottom)*

Focusing on innovative design since 1989, MODA is located in Atlanta's Midtown Arts District. A Smithsonian Institution affiliate, the museum's unique appreciation for creativity in architecture, technology, fashion, and more, delves into the inspirational and social impact of great design.

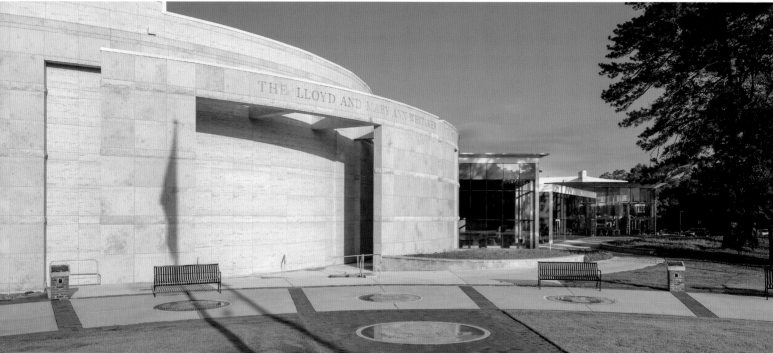

Atlanta History Center *(top and bottom)*

Significant Civil War exhibits, 19th-century dwellings, beautiful gardens, an extensive research center, and many other historic treasures are packed into the 33-acre experience that is the Atlanta History Center. Programs, lectures, events, and more will satisfy the curiosity of every history buff.

Locomotion Exhibit (top)

Atlanta's reputation as a major transportation hub evolved from the significant role of its railroad industry. The *Locomotion: Railroads and the Making of Atlanta!* exhibit at the Atlanta History Center, features the restored locomotive *Texas,* as well as stories from Meet the Past museum theatre characters.

Explore Atlanta (bottom)

From folk art to Native-American artifacts; from the world's largest Civil War exhibit to the history of barbecue, as well as influences of notable locals like golf icon, Bobby Jones, the Atlanta History Center is enlightening. Exhibits educate on growth and change that made Atlanta the vibrant city it is today.

Georgia's Rural History

Atlanta's oldest farmhouse, the Smith Family Farm is part of the Atlanta History Center. Many of the hands who worked the farm during the mid-1800s were enslaved people. This small, rustic cabin, moved here from Cliftondale, was indicative of the original slave quarters that did not survive.

Elegant Interiors *(above and right)*

Named for the swan-themed paintings and sculptures found throughout the mansion's interior, the Swan House was decorated by distinguished, 1930s interior designer, Ruby Ross Wood of New York City. Special tours of secret rooms and hidden collections are offered in addition to the general admission.

Wren's Nest *(above, left, and opposite)*

Famous for the *Uncle Remus* tales featuring Brer Rabbit, slave stories from his youth, author Joel Chandler Harris once lived in this enchanting 1870, Queen Anne-style home. Known as the Wren's Nest, the West End landmark is a museum and educational center focusing on African-American folklore.

Callanwolde Fine Arts Center

(top, bottom, and opposite)

This elegant, Tudor Revival-style mansion was home to Howard Candler, president of Coca-Cola from 1906 to 1923. Today, it is the city's premiere public arts and cultural center offering gallery exhibits, a summer jazz concert series, holiday events, and art education.

Governor's Mansion *(above and left)*

The 30-room, 24,000-square-foot mansion boasts marble floors, a sweeping staircase, and one of the most extensive collections of Federal Period furnishings in the United States. The library includes a first edition, signed copy of Margaret Mitchell's *Gone with the Wind*.

Governor's Mansion
(opposite top and bottom)

Designed by A. Thomas Bradbury, the stately, Greek Revival Governor's Mansion was built in 1967. Surrounded by 30, 24-foot-tall Doric columns, the home sits on a sprawling 18 acres, and its grounds are exquisitely landscaped. Tours are available throughout the year.

Jimmy Carter Presidential Center

Comprised of The Carter Center and the Jimmy Carter Presidential Library and Museum, Carter Presidential Center was founded in 1982. The center's focus is the advancement of human rights and alleviation of human suffering—ideals that would award the 39th President of the United States a Nobel Peace Prize.

Sightless Among Miracles *(top)*

Afflicted with river blindness, an African man is led by his younger counterpart in R.T. Wallen's moving sculpture, *Sightless Among Miracles*. Created in 1995, the statue, located on the grounds of the Carter Center, commemorates the selfless goal of the center to slow and eventually eradicate this disease.

Jimmy Carter Presidential Library and Museum *(bottom)*

An extensive collection of documents, photographs, and film, along with insightful exhibits, give a detailed look into the highest office in the U.S. The museum also includes a replica of the Oval Office and is run by the National Archives and Records Administration.

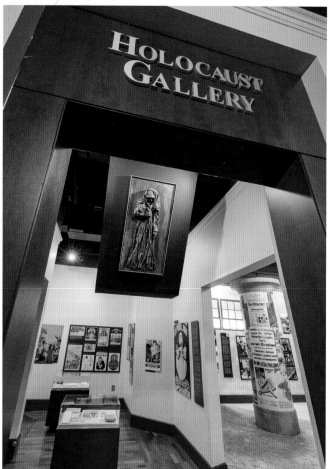

William Breman Jewish Heritage Museum *(above and left)*

Poignant exhibits display the heights of human oppression and resiliency of the human spirit that are so deeply rooted in Jewish heritage. It is this museum's noble mission to advance tolerance and understanding in order to prevent future generations from repeating such atrocities.

Martin Luther King, Jr. National Historic Site *(above)*

The gravesite of Dr. Martin Luther King, Jr. and his wife Coretta Scott King is surrounded by a peaceful reflecting pool at The King Center. The center, along with several related sites, comprise the Martin Luther King, Jr. National Historic Site, established in 1980.

A Treasured Landmark *(right)*

Dedicated to the vision of this extraordinary man to overcome social injustice through his principals of nonviolence, The King Center is one of Atlanta's most renowned landmarks. Founded in 1968, the center continues to advocate Dr. King's agenda of progress through peace.

Birthplace of a Leader *(above)*

A bronze plaque, embedded in the walkway of this Queen Anne-style home on Auburn Avenue, marks the birthplace of civil rights leader, Dr. Martin Luther King, Jr. The home, gravesite, and church comprise The Martin Luther King, Jr., National Historic Site.

Ebenezer Baptist Church *(left)*

Martin Luther King, Jr. delivered his first sermon at this church in 1947. Following in the footsteps of his father, he became an ordained minister which would shape his endeavors in the nonviolent pursuit of civil rights. He remained a co-minister with his father until his assassination in 1968.

Behold *(opposite)*

Across from Ebenezer Baptist Church in Peace Park, *Behold*, by sculptor Patrick Morelli was unveiled in 1990. Inspired by an ancient African ritual in which a new father utters, *"Behold the only thing greater than yourself,"* the bronze figure embodies the courage and spirt of Dr. Martin Luther King, Jr.

Margaret Mitchell House (*above*)

Pulitzer Prize winning author Margaret Mitchell penned the epic Civil War saga, *Gone with the Wind*, in apartment No. 1 of this Tudor Revival home on Crescent Avenue in Midtown. Built in 1899, the home is operated by the Atlanta History Center and is listed on the National Register of Historic Places.

Birthplace of an American Classic
(above and right)

Margaret Mitchell shared this small apartment with her husband John Marsh from 1925 to 1932. Along with the encouragement and editing skills of her husband, she would make a major contribution to American literature by authoring the gripping tale *Gone with the Wind*.

Oakland Cemetery *(above and opposite)*

Originally named Atlanta Graveyard, historic Oakland Cemetery started in 1850 with six acres. Mounting Civil War casualties would expand the cemetery to 48 acres. Featuring ornate mausoleums in various architectural styles, the cemetery was placed on the National Register of Historic Places in 1976.

Peaceful Garden Sanctuary *(left)*

A peaceful, botanical preserve—shade trees and unique sculpture are found throughout this historic cemetery. Located near the heart of downtown, it is the resting place of notable Atlantans such as pro golfer Bobby Jones and renowned author Margaret Mitchell as well as many of the city's first settlers.

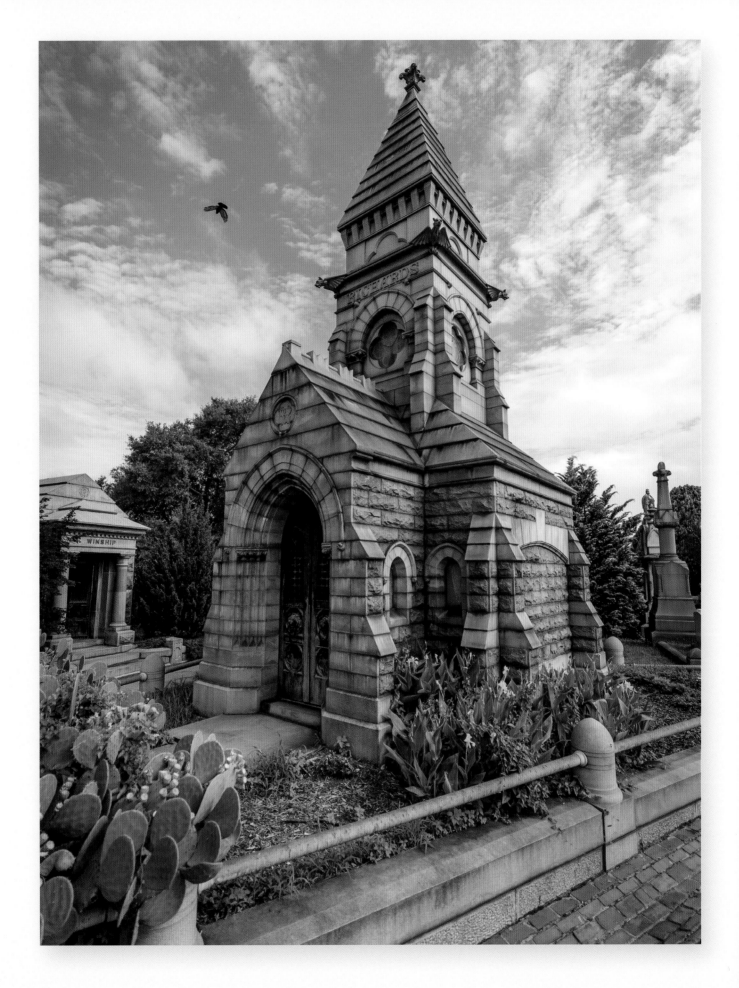

Peace Monument *(opposite)*

The Gate City Guard was the first Georgia company to do battle in the Civil War. When the war had ended, Captain J. F. Burke reinstated the company to become the first to secure the peace. Dedicated in 1911, the *Peace Monument* in Piedmont Park is a lasting tribute to reconciliation between the states.

Piedmont Park *(top and bottom)*

Based on a 1912 plan by the sons of famed landscape architect Frederick Law Olmsted, Piedmont Park is 211 acres of woodlands, wetlands, and sprawling open space. A favorite for bicyclists, fitness enthusiasts, and dog walkers, this urban playground is the center for summer concerts and festivals.

Piedmont Park Trails

A four-mile-long trail meanders through meadows and under shady trees as it loops its way around Piedmont Park. Skyline views, glimpses of the Atlanta Botanical Garden, and an unpaved portion that unveils the beauty of the wetlands are just some of the many features that make this trail so popular.

The Last Meter

In an agonizing quest for victory, runners race toward the finish in this sculpture by internationally renowned artist Eino. Created for the Centennial Olympic Games, *The Last Meter*, in Piedmont Park, depicts the final leg of a 5,000-meter race held at the 1976 Montreal Games, won by Lasse Virén of Finland.

Freedom Park (top)

Freedom Park exists as a result of persistent efforts by neighborhood protestors who, during the 1970s, fought against plans to include a major, four-lane highway through the area. Designated as an "art park" in 2008, it features many permanent and temporary creative sculptures.

Tree of Life (bottom)

Tree of Life, by sculptor Yvonne Domenge, is one of six individual works that, together, make up an original sculpture called *Interconnected*. Appearing in its entirety in Chicago in 2012, the piece was divided and installed in different cities across America, including here in Freedom Park.

One Woman Rising (opposite)

Freedom Park's permanent art collection includes the exuberant *One Woman Rising*. Sculpted by Phil Proctor and decorated by a team of talented painters, the 12-foot-tall, dancing female figure is internationally recognized as a symbol of overcoming violence against women and girls.

Dorothy Chapman Fuqua Conservatory
(above and left)

Desert and tropical plants are showcased among five areas of this 16,000-square-foot conservatory that opened in 1989 at the Atlanta Botanical Garden. Display areas include an Orangerie, a Desert House, a Tropical Rotunda, an amphibian display, and a special exhibits area.

Fuqua Orchid Center *(above and right)*

Part of the Fuqua Conservatory at the Atlanta Botanical Garden, the Fuqua Orchid Center includes two display houses that showcase more than 200 genera and 2,000 species of the orchid family. A separate laboratory allows visitors a glimpse at the conservation science being done here.

Mershon Hall *(opposite)*

A stately structure among the finely manicured beds of the Atlanta Botanical Garden, Mershon Hall was built in 2003. Located just off the Parterre, the building is used primarily for private events such as wedding receptions and business events, and also hosts concerts and large flower shows.

Imaginary Worlds *(above)*

A spectacular, 20-foot-tall dragon, made from more than 24,000 plants, is the largest mosaiculture sculpture in Atlanta Botanical Garden's *Imaginary Worlds: Once Upon a Time* exhibit. From peacocks to mermaids, magical creatures, made with over 200,000 plants, can be found both indoors and out.

Skyline Garden *(pages 112-113)*

Atlanta Botanical Garden's new 1.5-acre Skyline Garden opened in 2017. Bright seasonal blooms with a stunning city backdrop highlight this peaceful Midtown oasis designed by Spurlock Landscape Architects and 3.fromme DESIGN. This serene paradise has also become a popular, romantic wedding location.

Zoo Atlanta *(above)*

One of the oldest zoo's in the country, Zoo Atlanta began in 1889 as a road-side curiosity. Today, it is home to more than 1,000 animals, including giant pandas Lun Lun and Yang Yang who arrived from China in 1999. The more than 40-acre park is a leader in animal advocacy, preservation, and education.

Orangutans *(left)*

Three separate areas within 1.5 acres provide lots of swinging and climbing options for these marvelous creatures at Zoo Atlanta. Adult male orangutans can weigh up to 250 pounds and have an arm span of up to 9 feet. Highly endangered, these intelligent problem solvers live in the rainforests of Southeast Asia.

Sumatran Tiger *(left)*

A Sumatran tiger lurks in the brush of the *Asian Forest* habitat at Zoo Atlanta. Native to Sumatra in Indonesia, these powerful carnivores can weigh 200-300 pounds. Seen year-round, the zoo provides these endangered residents with a comfortable indoor environment to escape cold and rainy days.

Western Lowland Gorilla *(right)*

Characterized by a reddish-brown crest, the massive western lowland gorilla can be found deep in the rainforests of western Africa. Zoo Atlanta's *Ford African Rain Forest* habitat opened in 1988 and has since seen the birth of more than 20 gorillas. It now has the largest population of gorillas in North America.

Georgia Tech *(above and opposite)*

With a campus stretching across 400 acres in downtown Atlanta, Georgia Tech is highly ranked for excellence in academics, athletics, diversity, innovation, and more. Founded in 1885 and with a student enrollment of over 25,000, it is one of the top research universities in the United States.

Georgia State University
(pages 118-119)

Located near Woodruff Park, Georgia State University has a student population of over 51,000. The university is comprised of 10 colleges and schools, with focuses on business, law, nursing, biomedical, and more. It also has study abroad opportunities worldwide.

Georgia State Football *(above)*

Georgia State's Football program was launched in 2008, and in 2010 the Panthers played their first game. Their 25,000-seat stadium was built in 1996 for the Summer Olympic Games. Converted to Turner Field, it was home of MLB's Atlanta Braves until 2016 when it became Georgia State Stadium.

College Football Hall of Fame
(opposite top)

The greatest college football stars are celebrated at the College Football Hall of Fame. Founded in 1951, the Hall opened in Ohio in 1978, moved to Indiana in 1995, and settled here in Atlanta in 2014. The facility also hosts events and community outreach programs

Hall of Fame Icons
(opposite bottom)

A wall of 768 helmets, three stories high, are found in this 95,000-square-foot, state-of-the-art Hall of Fame that honors football's best amateur players. Here, college football history comes alive with interactive exhibits, galleries, and a 47-yard football field.

Mercedes-Benz Stadium *(above)*

Beauty, functionality, and sustainability come together in one of the world's most impressive athletic stadiums. Home to the NFL's Atlanta Falcons, visitors to the $1.6-billion-dollar stadium are greeted by a colossal, 65-foot-wide, 4-story-tall, stainless steel falcon created by sculptor Gábor Miklós Szöke.

From Athletics to Art *(opposite top)*

Mercedes-Benz Stadium features an expansive collection of contemporary art, inside and out. The collection, acquired in partnership with the Savannah College of Art and Design, features the inspirational works of 54 local and international artists that focus on both athletics and the history of Atlanta.

State Farm Arena *(opposite bottom)*

Adjacent to Mercedes-Benz Stadium, State Farm Arena is home to the NBA's Atlanta Hawks and WMBA's Atlanta Dream. It opened in 2018 after undergoing the second most extensive renovation in NBA history. A premier entertainment venue, millions of visitors attend close to 200 events annually.

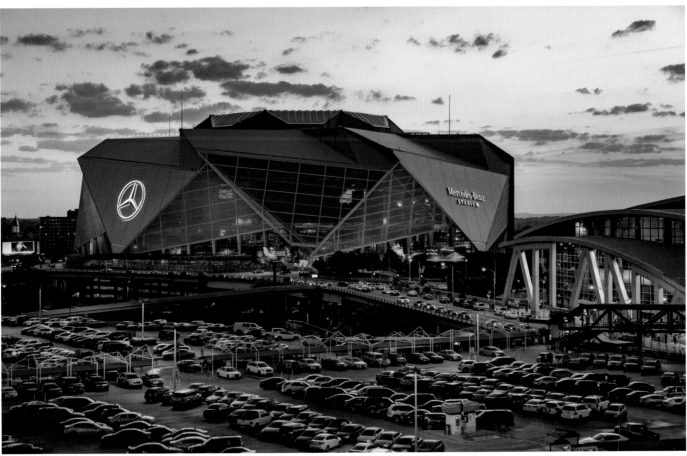

Atlanta United *(above and left)*

With attendance topping 1 million, the Atlanta United plays to a packed house under the retractable roof of their home venue, Mercedes-Benz Stadium. Joining Major League Soccer in 2017, the club begins each game by driving a large golden spike into a platform—a salute to the city's railroad heritage.

SunTrust Park *(opposite top and bottom)*

The new home of MLB's Atlanta Braves. This 41,000-seat stadium is located between the Omni Hotel and The Battery Atlanta—a major shopping and entertainment area. With an emphasis on accessibility, the new state-of-the-art stadium is enhanced with more parking and three new pedestrian bridges.

SunTrust Park *(top)*

Designed with line of sight in mind, the new SunTrust Park provides every fan with the best seat in the house. Its 41,000 seats include 4,000 premium seats in the SunTrust Club, Delta SKY360 Club, and Terrace Club. Kiosks "rent" free gloves to hopeful Braves fans in foul-ball and home-run areas.

Hank Aaron Statue *(bottom and opposite)*

Surrounded by the historical icons of MLB's Atlanta Braves in SunTrust Park's Monument Garden, the statue of "the greatest Brave of all time" was unveiled in 2017. Renowned Atlanta-based artist Ross Rossin captured the moment when Hank Aaron surpassed Babe Ruth's home-run record on April 8, 1974.

Chris Hamilton has photographed all over the world, but Atlanta is his home. With roots in WV and an education from Clemson, Chris headed to the big city and enrolled in photography at the Art Institute of Atlanta. "Atlanta is a different city than even 10 years ago and it's exciting. It's a city of connected neighborhoods, each with its own vibe." Chris loves immersing himself into whatever he is photographing. His interests include architecture, sports, children, people, and landscapes, especially the beach. He's been the official photographer for the Atlanta Braves, the Paralympics, and the American Cancer Society. His photographs have been featured in the High Museum of Art, on the pages of *Sports Illustrated*, and on billboards in Times Square. To see more of his work, visit the Chris Hamilton Photography website at www.hamphoto.com.

Award-winning graphic designer, **Sara Day**, never ceases to be inspired by the beauty and unique qualities of regions throughout the United States. A native of Gloucester, Massachusetts, Sara has enjoyed a long career working with publishers, photographers, and advertising agencies. She now resides in Vero Beach, Florida, where she continues to use her talents to create exquisite photo journals and high-end promotional materials. To see more, visit sypdesign.com and www.twinlightspub.com.